BLAST OFF
with Ellen Ochoa!

Margarita González-Jensen
and Peter Rillero

Photo Credits

4 right, 7, 9, 23 bottom right NASA/Digital Vision
All other photos, courtesy of NASA
Each child provided his or her photo

© 1999 by Rigby,
a division of Reed Elsevier Inc.
1000 Hart Rd.
Barrington, IL 60010-2627

Executive Editor: Lynelle H. Morgenthaler
Design assistance provided by Herman Adler Design Group

All rights reserved. No part of this publication
may be reproduced or transmitted in any form
or by any means, electronic or mechanical,
including photocopying, recording, taping, or
any information storage and retrieval system,
without permission in writing from the publisher.

04 03 02 01
10 9 8 7 6 5

Printed in Singapore

ISBN 0-7635-5713-7

Crew of shuttle Discovery; Ellen Ochoa on far right

Being an astronaut is a job that's out of this world! Have you ever wondered what it's like to be an astronaut? The children in this book had a chance to ask Ellen Ochoa themselves. She knows all about astronauts—she is one!

What were your favorite things to do as a little girl?
Mozelle Moreno, Texas

Ellen Ochoa: I enjoyed reading adventure stories about girls. I also liked watching the astronauts on their trip to the moon. I took piano and flute lessons. I even took my flute into space!

Ochoa playing flute in space

First U.S. astronaut on the moon

Why did you want to be an astronaut?
Nikkie Patel, Idaho

Ellen Ochoa: Blasting off into space, being weightless, and seeing Earth from space sounded exciting. I also wanted to work with a team in a space lab. I knew I could do these things as an astronaut.

Ochoa blasts off

Ochoa's team, weightless

What did you study in school?
Blanca Farias, Idaho

Ellen Ochoa: I studied math and science, just like you do. I loved to read so much, my mother had to make me go to sleep at night. I also took ballet and gymnastics lessons after school.

Ochoa as a young child

What are the jobs of an astronaut?

Kristina Vega, Arizona

Ellen Ochoa: Astronauts control the space shuttle and do science experiments. They put objects called satellites into space so that the satellites circle Earth. Sometimes they take space walks.

A satellite circling the Earth

What stuff did you train on in astronaut school?
Mitch DiMauro, Ohio

Ellen Ochoa: We had classes that taught us how to run engines, radios, computers, and other equipment on the space shuttle. We practiced spacewalking in a large pool. We also trained for the specific jobs we would have on the space shuttle.

Ochoa in pool, training for water landing

Capturing a satellite

What was your favorite part of training?

Jessica Granados, Texas

Ellen Ochoa: I liked learning certain jobs that are done in space. For example, we put small satellites into space and captured them back. The crew worked together on this tricky move. I caught them with a big arm run by computer!

What was your favorite food in space?
Tanvi Patel, Idaho

Ellen Ochoa: I liked steaks, spaghetti, asparagus, and cheese macaroni. Tortillas were great space food. They packed flat and were easy to eat—no crumbs! For a quick snack, we spread tuna salad or peanut butter on them.

An astronaut's meal

How did you go to the bathroom?

William Rillero, Ohio

Sade McCann, Ohio

Ellen Ochoa: Straps helped to keep us from floating away while using the bathroom! Since we couldn't count on gravity, a machine blew air that sent the waste into a tank.

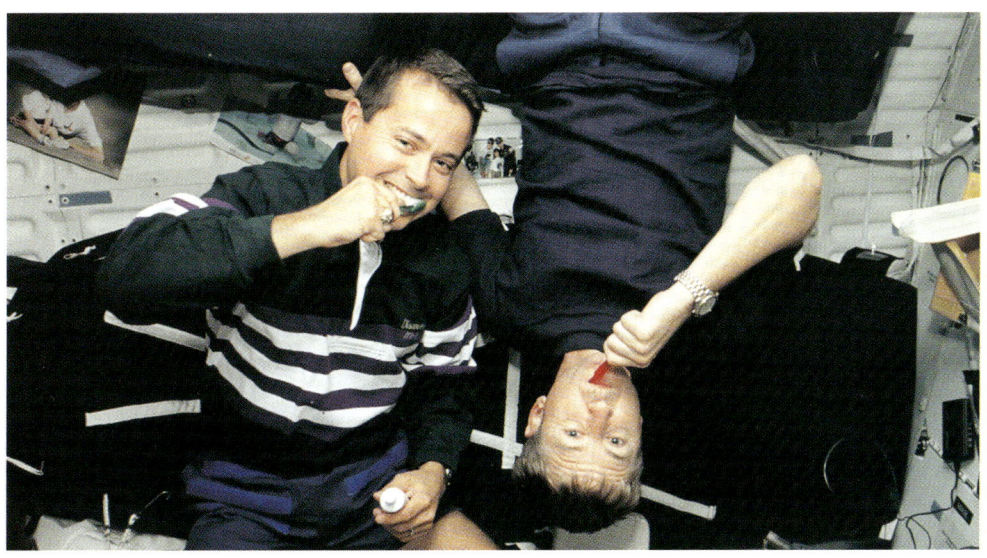

Astronauts brushing their teeth

What did Earth look like from space?

Jardiel Dominguez, Idaho

Ellen Ochoa: Earth was always changing from day to night to day again. Also, it looked different depending on whether we were over oceans, deserts, mountains, or cities. It was very beautiful!

Earth at day

Earth at night

VIEWS OF THE EARTH FROM SPACE

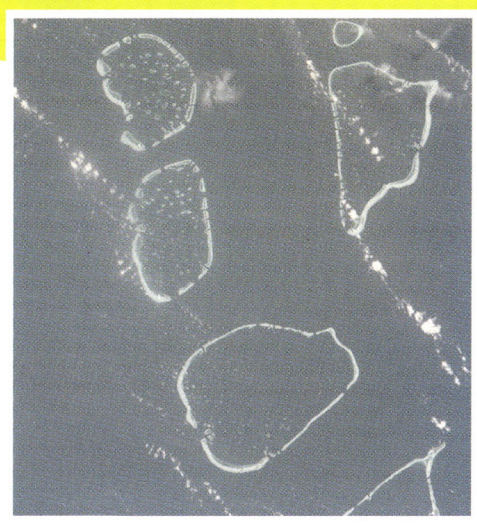
Ocean

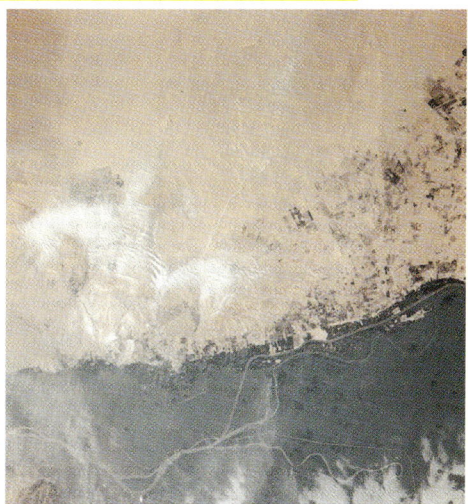
Desert

Mountains

New York city

13

What kind of clothes did you wear?

Edid Díaz, Arizona

Ellen Ochoa: We usually wore knit shirts and pants with velcro strips to hold equipment. We wore socks but no shoes. We had space suits to wear if we needed them.

Ochoa in knit shirt and pants

Ochoa in space suit

Astronauts floating with tools tacked down

How did it feel to be in space?
Chelsea McGuire, Arizona

Ellen Ochoa: It was fun to float in any position, like upside down, or to go feet first up stairs. But working was difficult since anything I laid down floated away! I always had to attach my tools to something.

15

Shuttle Discovery landing

What kind of spaceship did you ride in?
Allison Hylant, Ohio

Ellen Ochoa: It was called the space shuttle. The shuttle lands like an airplane, so it can be used many times. It carries up to seven people and everything they need to live and work. Its longest flight was 18 days.

SPACE SHUTTLE DIAGRAM

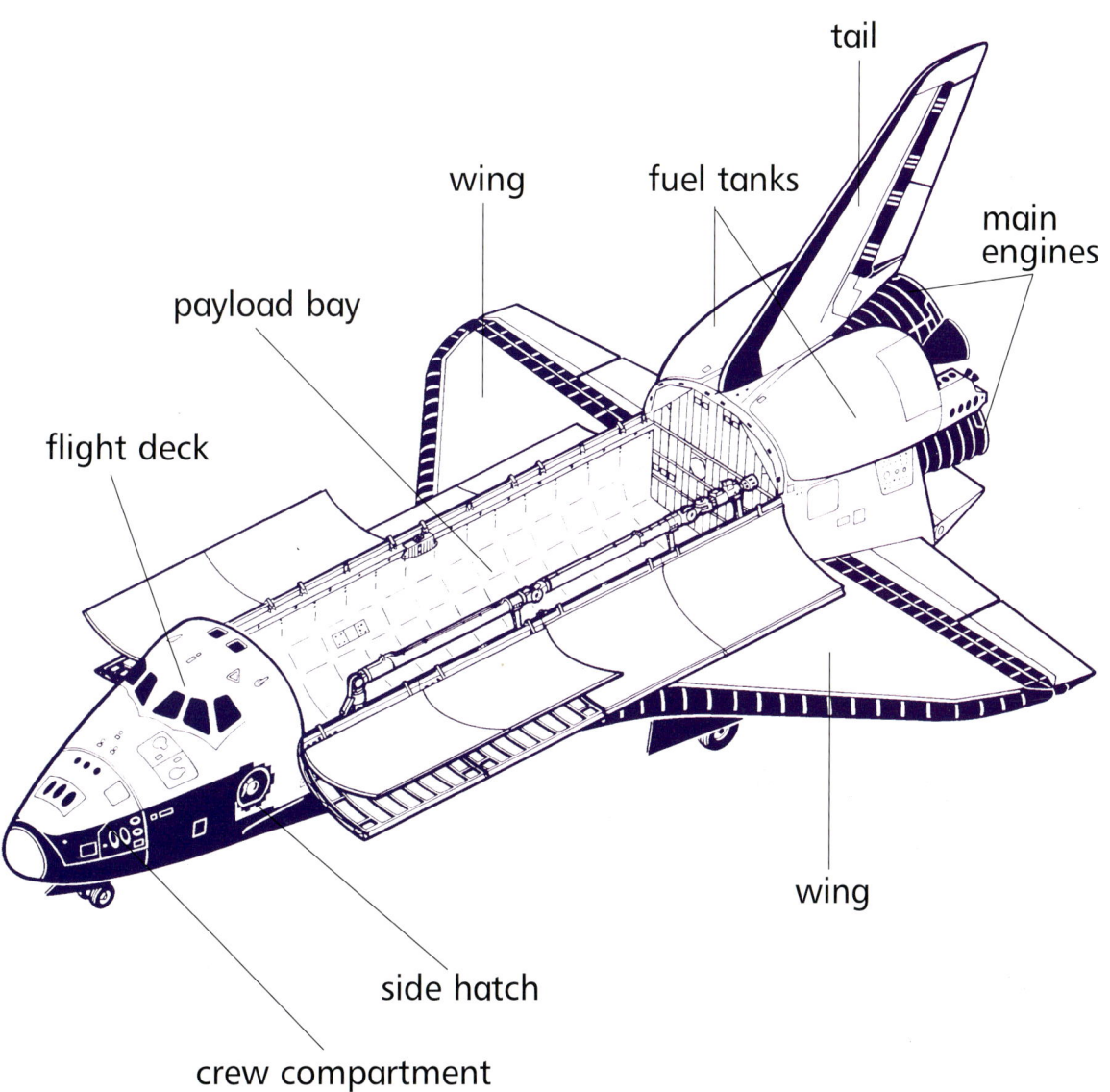

> The first time you rode in a rocket, were you afraid?
>
> Jessica Madregal-Guerrero, Idaho

Ellen Ochoa: Although I knew things could go wrong, I wasn't afraid. Many people had worked hard making it as safe as possible. I just kept thinking about what I needed to do. I remember being very excited!

Ochoa's first space flight

Shuttle circling the Earth

How long did it take to get to space?

Amy Srimoukda, Idaho

Ellen Ochoa: It took eight and a half minutes to get from the launchpad to the place where we started circling Earth. This circling is called an orbit and is 180 miles above the ground. We go around Earth at 17,500 miles per hour!

Have you been to Mars?
Jonathen Morawski, Michigan

Ellen Ochoa: No one has been to Mars yet—or any other planet. But over 25 years ago, 12 people walked on the moon. Perhaps you can go to Mars some day!

Mars

Walking on the moon

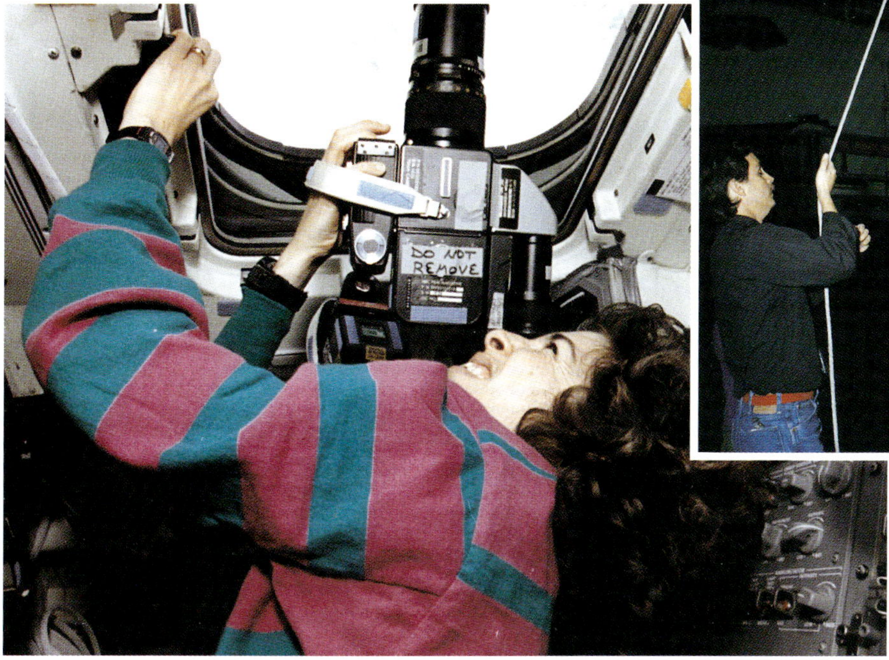

Ochoa at work

Do you like being an astronaut?
Dianira Rios, Idaho

Ellen Ochoa: Yes, it's a great job! Being an astronaut takes a lot of hard work, but it's full of amazing experiences!

TIME LINES

Ellen Ochoa

1958
Born May 10 in California.

1968
Started playing flute.

1975
Graduated Grossmont High School.

| 1955 | 1960 | 1965 | 1970 | 1975 |

1957
First satellite in space: Sputnik 1

1961
First person in space (April): Yuri A. Gagarin
First U.S. citizen in space (May): Alan Shepard

1969
First people on Moon: Apollo 11

1976
Viking landed on Mars and sent photos.

Space Exploration

22

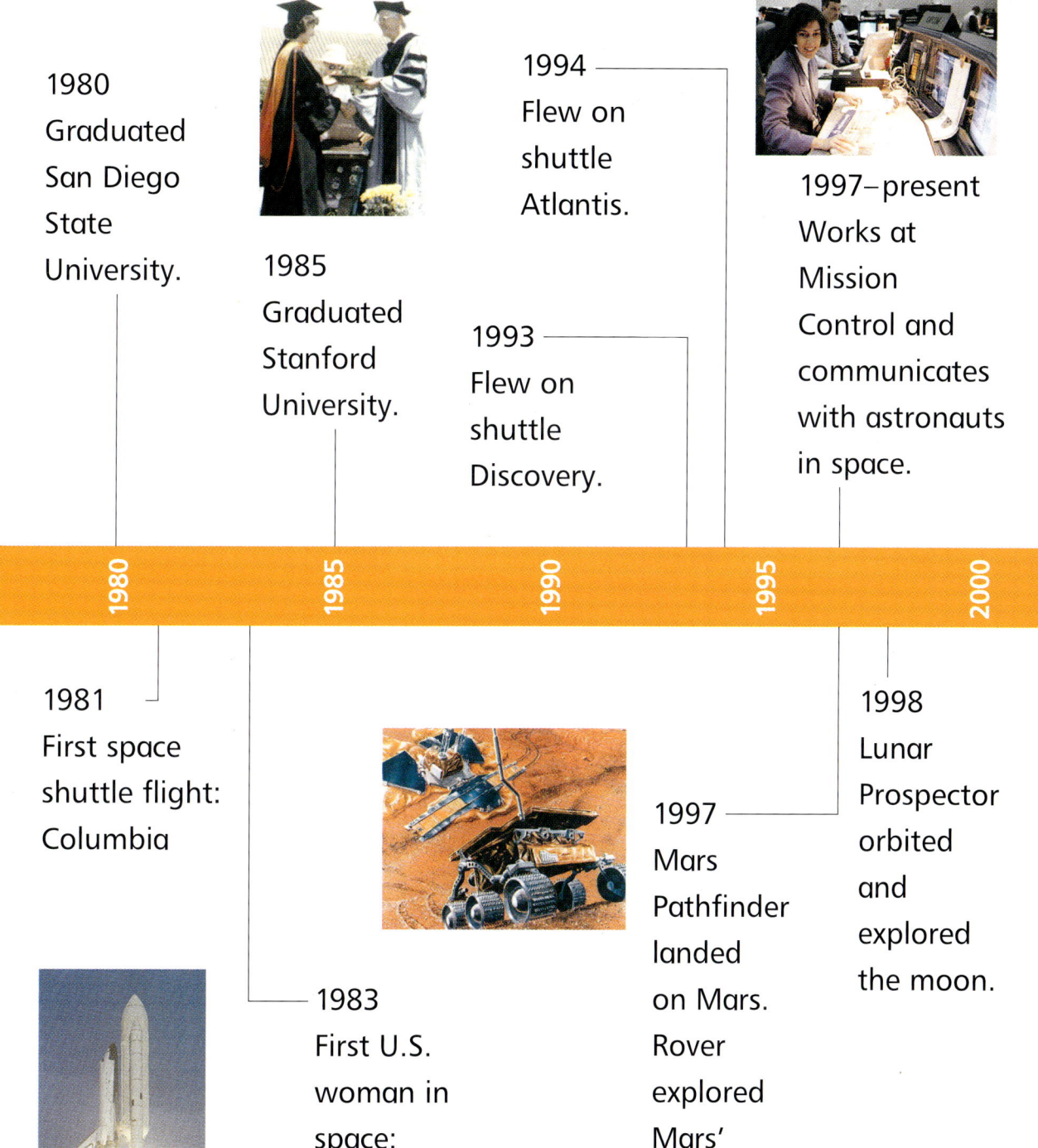

1980 Graduated San Diego State University.

1985 Graduated Stanford University.

1994 Flew on shuttle Atlantis.

1993 Flew on shuttle Discovery.

1997–present Works at Mission Control and communicates with astronauts in space.

1981 First space shuttle flight: Columbia

1983 First U.S. woman in space: Sally K. Ride

1997 Mars Pathfinder landed on Mars. Rover explored Mars' landscape.

1998 Lunar Prospector orbited and explored the moon.

A MESSAGE FROM ELLEN OCHOA

Magic doesn't make dreams come true. Setting goals does. As a child, I didn't know I would become an astronaut, but I always set goals. Get a good education and believe in yourself. That's how I became a NASA astronaut. The future is yours—think big!